A Guide to
AMERICAN STATES
★ ★ ★ ★ ★

Minnesota

THE NORTH STAR STATE

MEDIA ENHANCED BOOKS
AV²
BY WEIGL
ADDED VALUE • AUDIO VISUAL

www.av2books.com

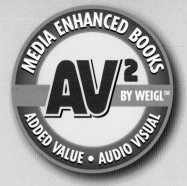

AV² provides enriched content that supplements and complements this book. Weigl's AV² books strive to create inspired learning and engage young minds in a total learning experience.

Your AV² Media Enhanced books come alive with...

Audio
Listen to sections of the book read aloud.

Key Words
Study vocabulary, and complete a matching word activity.

Video
Watch informative video clips.

Quizzes
Test your knowledge.

Embedded Weblinks
Gain additional information for research.

Slide Show
View images and captions, and prepare a presentation.

Try This!
Complete activities and hands-on experiments.

... and much, much more!

Go to **www.av2books.com**, and enter this book's unique code.

BOOK CODE

W 2 6 2 1 1 1

AV² by Weigl brings you media enhanced books that support active learning.

Published by AV² by Weigl
350 5th Avenue, 59th Floor
New York, NY 10118
Website: www.av2books.com   www.weigl.com

Library of Congress Cataloging-in-Publication Data

Purslow, Neil.
 Minnesota / Neil Purslow.
    p. cm. -- (A guide to American states)
 Includes index.
 ISBN 978-1-61690-795-2 (hardcover : alk. paper) -- ISBN 978-1-61690-471-5 (online)
1. Minnesota--Juvenile literature. I. Title.
 F606.3.P875 2011
 977.6--dc23
                      2011018335

Printed in the United States of America in North Mankato, Minnesota

052011
WEP180511

Project Coordinator Jordan McGill
Art Director Terry Paulhus

Contents

Minneapolis is located on the shores of the Mississippi River. It is the largest city in Minnesota.

Introduction

Minnesota is famous for its many lakes. One of the state's nicknames is Land of 10,000 Lakes, but there are actually more than 12,000. With so many lakes, fishing and canoeing are popular recreational sports. Along Minnesota's lakeshores are a variety of cottages, beaches, tourist camps, and resorts. In addition to its lakes, the state's plentiful resources include rivers, forests, minerals, and fertile soil. These resources have allowed a diverse economy to evolve over the years. Fur trapping, **flour milling**, and lumbering were early industries to develop in Minnesota. Iron-ore mining has been vital to the northern part of the state. Today, food processing, particularly of corn and dairy products, and other manufacturing contribute greatly to the state's wealth.

Minnesota's rich agricultural history rests on its fertile soil. Agriculture is still an important industry in the state.

The Boundary Waters Canoe Area Wilderness in northeast Minnesota is the most visited wilderness in the United States. It contains more than 1,000 beautiful lakes and streams.

In addition to the thousands of lakes, the natural landscape of Minnesota is etched in valleys, prairies, wilderness areas, high bluffs, and rocky shores. One small part of Minnesota extends farther north than any other state in the country except Alaska.

About one out of every two Minnesotans lives within the greater **metropolitan area** of Minneapolis and St. Paul, which together are known as the Twin Cities. These neighboring cities straddle the Mississippi River. Minneapolis, which means "city of water," is known for its clean, modern look and its beautiful lakes and parks. The state's largest city, it has 16 lakes as well as lagoons, other wetlands, and more than 150 parks within its limits. St. Paul traces its roots to a 19th-century settlement called Pig's Eye. It has since grown to become Minnesota's capital and second largest city.

Where Is Minnesota?

Minnesota is one of 13 states that share a border with Canada. It is the 12ᵗʰ largest state in total area. Minnesota is 358 miles wide at its widest point and 406 miles long from north to south. Minnesota is located in the north-central United States. The Canadian provinces of Manitoba and Ontario are its neighbors to the north. North Dakota and South Dakota are to the west. Iowa is to the south, and Wisconsin and Lake Superior are to the east.

Lake Itasca in northwest Minnesota is the source of the Mississippi River. The lake is located in Itasca State Park.

Minnesota gets its name from the Dakota Indian word *minisota*, which means "water that reflects the sky." Indeed, water is an important part of Minnesota. The state's license plates read "10,000 Lakes," and the state has more shoreline than the states of California, Florida, and Hawaii combined. In addition, the Mississippi River, which is one of the world's longest rivers, begins at Lake Itasca in northern Minnesota. The state also has many striking waterfalls.

Most people travel to Minnesota by air or road. A network of highways totaling 12,000 miles crisscrosses the state. The state also boasts nine commercial airports. The largest airport in Minnesota is the Minneapolis–St. Paul International Airport, which serves more than 30 million travelers each year.

The beautiful Minnehaha Falls are located in Minnehaha Park in Minneapolis. The 193-acre park is one of the city's most popular parks.

Minnesota has a few nicknames. In addition to its official name, the North Star State, it is also the Gopher State and the Bread and Butter State.

The state flag features a wreath surrounding the state seal. Three dates appear on the wreath. They are 1819, for when Fort Snelling was founded, 1858, for when Minnesota joined the Union, and 1893, for when the flag was adopted.

Greyhound Lines, a company that provides bus transportation between cities, began operation in Minnesota in 1914. The first route took miners from Hibbing to several nearby iron mines.

The twin port of Duluth and Superior, Wisconsin, located at the western edge of Lake Superior, is the farthest inland water port in the world. The port is 2,300 miles west of the Atlantic Ocean. Oceangoing ships reach it by using the St. Lawrence Seaway, traveling up the St. Lawrence River and through the Great Lakes.

Minnesota claims more boats per person than any other state. One person in six owns a boat in Minnesota.

Mapping Minnesota

Minnesota's largest cities are located in the eastern part of the state. These include Minneapolis, St. Paul, and Bloomington. The northern part of the state is much less densely populated than the southern part. The state has more than 6,500 rivers and streams. In addition to the Mississippi River, other notable waterways include the Red River of the North, on the western border, the St. Croix River, on the east, and the Minnesota River.

Sites and Symbols

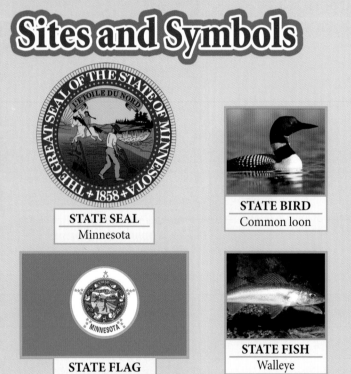

STATE SEAL
Minnesota

STATE BIRD
Common loon

STATE FLOWER
Pink and white lady's slipper

STATE FLAG
Minnesota

STATE FISH
Walleye

STATE TREE
Red or Norway pine

Nickname The North Star State

Motto *L'Etoile du Nord*
(The Star of the North)

Song "Hail Minnesota" by Truman E. Rickard and Arthur E. Upson

Entered the Union May 11, 1858, as the 32nd state

Capital St. Paul

Population (2010 Census) 5,303,925
Ranked 21st state

Winnipeg
Steinbach
MANITOBA

ONTARIO

International Falls
South International Falls

Thief River Falls

Grand Forks
Crookston

Mayville

Bemidji

Virginia

Hibbing

Silver Bay

MINNESOTA

Grand Rapids

Two Harbors

Fargo

Detroit Lakes
Perham

Duluth
Cloquet
Superior

Ashland

NORTH DAKOTA

Wadena
Fergus Falls
Staples

Brainerd

MICHIGAN
Bessemer

Hurley

Little Falls

Pine City

WISCONSIN

Alexandria

Sisseton

Morris

St. Cloud

Ladysmith
Barron
Tomahawk

Ortonville
Benson

Ramsey
Fridley

Bloomer
Chippewa Falls
Merrill
Wausau

Watertown

Montevideo
Willmar

Minneapolis **St. Paul**

SOUTH DAKOTA

Bloomington

Lakeville
Northfield
Red Wing

Eau Claire

Marshall
Tracy
Springfield

New Ulm
Mankato

Faribault
Owatonna

Winona

Rochester
Stewartville

Luverne
Worthington
Fairmont

Austin
Albert Lea

Map Scale
0   100 Miles

N

LEGEND
— Road
— River
⭐ State Capital
• City
▢ Minnesota
— State Border

Sioux Falls
Canton
Sheldon
Spencer
Emmetsburg
Garner
Mason City
Charles City

IOWA

STATE CAPITAL

When the Minnesota Territory was organized in 1849, St. Paul became the territorial capital. When Minnesota was granted statehood in 1858, that city became the state capital.

United States

Hawai'i Alaska

Minnesota

The Land

Minnesota is made up of two major natural regions. In the northeastern corner is the Superior Upland. This region is a forested area of lakes, peat **bogs**, and ridges. Long ago, **glaciers** scraped away most of the soil in this part of the state. Valuable beds of iron ore lie beneath the land surface. The other major land region in Minnesota is the Central Lowland. It covers the largest part of the state. This area was sculpted by glaciers and is generally flat, with some hills and valleys. All of this portion of Minnesota was once the floor of prehistoric Lake Agassiz. This lake was created 8,000 years ago when glacier ice melted. As the lake dried up, it left behind rich soil.

LAKE SUPERIOR

Lake Superior makes up Minnesota's northeast border. The lakeshore is characterized by rugged cliffs, rock-filled pools, woods, and waterfalls.

CENTRAL LOWLAND

Much of the Central Lowland is a fertile plain with rolling prairie, hills, and valleys.

SUPERIOR UPLAND

The Superior Upland, in the northeastern part of the state, has rolling hills and forests.

The Superior Upland drops hundreds of feet at the Lake Superior shoreline, creating amazing waterfalls.

The northwestern portion of the state is part of the Red River Valley. The river is more than 545 miles long and runs from Breckenridge in the south to Lake Winnipeg, in Canada, in the north.

The highest point in Minnesota is Eagle Mountain, at 2,301 feet. It is located in the northeastern part of the state and is surrounded by beautiful parks.

Superior National Forest and Boundary Water Canoe Area Wilderness, which lies within the forest, are natural tourist attractions. There are many plants and animals, and visitors can camp, hike, boat, and fish.

NERSTRAND–BIG WOODS STATE PARK

This state park, which contains the Hidden Falls Waterfall, is on the site of the "Big Woods," a vast stretch of trees that settlers found when they arrived in the 1850s.

Minneapolis averages about 47 inches of snow each year.

Climate

Minnesota's climate tends to be extreme. Warm summer temperatures average 70° Fahrenheit in the southern part of the state, and cold winter readings hover around 6° F in the north. The thermometer plunges to subzero temperatures during cold snaps in winter. On the other hand, heat waves are common occurrences in summer. The average annual precipitation ranges from 34 inches in the southeast to only 19 inches in the northwest.

The hottest temperature on record in Minnesota is 114° F, set at Beardsley on July 29, 1917 and at Moorhead on July 6, 1936. The coldest temperature on record is −60° F, set near Tower on February 2, 1996.

Average Annual Precipitation Across Minnesota

The average annual precipitation varies for different cities across Minnesota. Why might Grand Meadow get so much more rainfall than Karlstad?

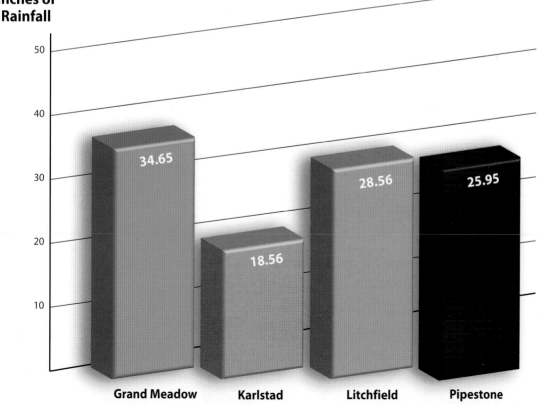

Inches of Rainfall

	Grand Meadow	Karlstad	Litchfield	Pipestone
	34.65	18.56	28.56	25.95

Natural Resources

Minnesota sits on huge reserves of iron ore, a mineral used to make steel. The iron ore is mined from both underground mines and **open-pit mines**, near the surface. These mines account for about 90 percent of the state's total mineral income. Minnesota is the largest producer of iron ore in the United States.

The Mesabi Range in northeast Minnesota contains some of the richest deposits of iron ore in the world.

Long ago, two-thirds of the state was covered with needle-leaf and hardwood forests. During the 1800s, the lumber industry was a central part of the state's economy. The forests were extensively logged and cleared for farms, however, and production fell off in the early 1900s. Today, only about one-third of Minnesota is still covered in forest. Most of the wood harvested by the state's forest industries is used to make wood products or to produce pulp and paper.

Logs from Minnesota's forests are used to make paper, pulp, furniture, and construction materials.

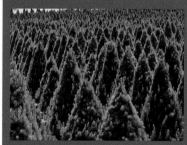

Plants

Coniferous forests once covered the northeastern third of the state. Logging in the region in the 1800s removed huge amounts of valuable pine from these forests. The regrowth of the forests included birch, poplar, and other trees. The other two-thirds of the land consisted mainly of **deciduous forests** and tall-grass prairie. When settlers from other parts of the United States arrived in what is now Minnesota, they turned much of the prairies into farms. A belt of deciduous forest known as the Big Woods still extends from the southeastern part of the state to the Canadian border. In this forest grow oak, maple, and basswood. Ash, elm, cottonwood, and box elder grow along the forest's stream valleys.

Minnesota has many beautiful wildflowers. They include the blue-eyed grass, pasqueflower, blazing star, and Northern blue flag. Prairie lilies, coneflowers, and pasture roses grow on the state's prairies.

NORWAY PINE

The Norway pine, or red pine, is Minnesota's state tree. It has reddish brown bark and generally grows to 100 feet tall.

PINK AND WHITE LADY'S SLIPPER

The pink and white lady's slipper is the state flower. It is a rare wildflower that grows slowly, taking up to 16 years to produce its first flower.

WILD RICE

The wild rice plant grows in shallow bodies of water. It produces a nutty-flavored seed eaten by both people and waterfowl.

PASQUEFLOWER

This wildflower is one of the first flowers that blooms in the spring on the Minnesota prairies.

Animals

Minnesota's northern forests are home to black bears, timber wolves, moose, and other large mammals. White-tailed deer are very common across the state. Smaller mammals such as raccoons, woodchucks, muskrats, mink, and skunks also live throughout the state. Common birds in the state include the cardinal, goldfinch, bluebird, and a small songbird called the white-breasted nuthatch. In recent years, Minnesota has seen an increase in the population of several types of birds that had been becoming more scarce. These include the wild turkey, tundra swan, trumpeter swan, sandhill crane, bald eagle, and peregrine falcon.

There are 14 species of frogs and toads in Minnesota and seven species of salamanders, including the spotted and tiger varieties. Only two venomous snakes can be found in the state, the massasauga and the timber rattlesnake.

MONARCH BUTTERFLY

The monarch butterfly is Minnesota's state butterfly. It spends the summer in Minnesota, then travels south to a warmer place for the winter.

BLACK BEAR

The black bear is the largest mammal in Minnesota. An adult male can weigh up to 500 pounds.

WOODCHUCK

Woodchucks are found in both rural and urban areas. They eat a variety of vegetables, grasses, and legumes.

COMMON LOON

The common loon is Minnesota's state bird. It is found on lakes throughout northeastern and central Minnesota.

During the summer, a type of grasshopper called the katydid is found throughout the state. The name "katydid" comes from the sound the males make to attract the females.

Gophers are common in the prairies of Minnesota. They spend most of their lives underground and are known for tearing up crops and gardens.

Peregrine falcons are fairly rare, but some of these birds can be seen nesting and flying in the Minneapolis–St. Paul area.

Fishing is a popular sport in Minnesota. The state's lakes and rivers are full of such fish as perch, bass, trout, catfish, and sturgeon.

Tourism

Minnesota's lakes, cottages, and summer weather bring tourists from all over the United States. Many come to enjoy the relaxed atmosphere. Others come for the recreational activities, such as boating, fishing, and swimming. The Winterfest in Duluth, the Winter Carnival in St. Paul, and the John Beargrease Sled Dog Marathon draw crowds in winter. The marathon is a 390-mile dogsled race from Duluth to the north shore of Lake Superior and back.

Minnesota's Voyageurs National Park and other sites managed by the National Park Service or the U.S. Forest Service are favorite destinations for campers. One of the largest national forests in the United States is Superior National Forest in the northeastern part of the state. It includes Winnibigoshish, Leech, and Cass lakes. Minnesota also has 66 state parks, six state recreation areas, and eight scenic waysides.

MALL OF AMERICA

The Mall of America, in Bloomington, is the nation's largest retail and entertainment complex. It contains a large indoor amusement park, an aquarium, a golf course, and more than 500 stores.

VOYAGEURS NATIONAL PARK

This national park was named for the French fur traders once active in the area. Visitors can camp and hike as well as boat and fish in the park's many lakes.

MINNEAPOLIS SCULPTURE GARDEN

The Minneapolis Sculpture Garden is one of the largest urban sculpture gardens in the United States. Its centerpiece is *Spoonbridge and Cherry*, a piece created by Claes Oldenburg and Coosje van Bruggen in the 1980s.

GRAND PORTAGE NATIONAL MONUMENT

Grand Portage National Monument is a reconstructed trading post in the northeastern corner of the state. Park staff and volunteers dress in period costume and teach visitors about what life was like at the old post.

The state's huge iron-ore open-pit mines are very popular tourist attractions.

At the International Wolf Center in Ely, visitors can learn all about how wolves live and communicate with each other.

Icebox Days in International Falls is a four-day event celebrating winter with activities such as snow sculpting and frozen turkey bowling.

The SPAM® Museum in Austin is dedicated to the meat product developed at the Hormel Foods plant in 1937.

Industry

Wheat once dominated Minnesota's agricultural economy. Although much wheat is still grown in Minnesota, corn and dairy farming have replaced it in importance. Corn is produced primarily as feed for pigs and cows. Dairy farms are found in the hilly southeastern and central portions of the state. Other leading farm products in Minnesota include soybeans, hay, sugar beets, potatoes, barley, hogs, cattle, chickens, and sheep.

Industries in Minnesota
Value of Goods and Services in Millions of Dollars

While manufacturing is important in Minnesota, the area of finance, insurance, and real estate contributes more to the state's economy. Other types of service industries, which provide services for people rather than actual products, are also important to the state's economy. What types of services are provided by the health-care industry and the people who work in it?

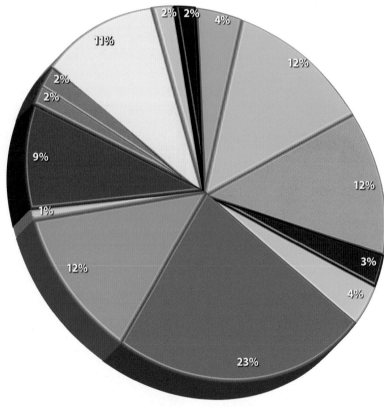

LEGEND

▪	Agriculture, Forestry, and Fishing	$5,276
✳	Mining	$388
■	Utilities	$4,240
▪	Construction	$10,596
▪	Manufacturing	$31,557
▪	Wholesale and Retail Trade	$31,108
■	Transportation	$6,696
▪	Media and Entertainment	$11,643
▪	Finance, Insurance, and Real Estate	$60,535
▪	Professional and Technical Services	$32,117
▪	Education	$2,472
■	Health Care	$23,435
▪	Hotels and Restaurants	$6,207
■	Other Services	$6,468
▪	Government	$27,954

TOTAL $260,692

*Less than 1%. Percentages may not add to 100 because of rounding.

Manufacturing is another important part of the state's economy. Food processing and the manufacture of machinery and high-technology equipment are all prominent. The state's food-processing industries pack meat, process dairy products, mill grain, and package fruits and vegetables. One of the state's best-known companies is 3M, which began in 1902 as the Minnesota Mining and Manufacturing Company. The company, which has its headquarters in St. Paul, makes a wide range of products, including adhesive tape, photographic film, electronics and medical materials, and Post-It brand notepads. General Mills, headquartered in Golden Valley, is a major producer of cereal and other food products. In addition, iron-ore mining and forestry continue to be important industries in Minnesota.

Minnesota has more than 80,000 farms. Livestock raised includes cattle, hogs, bison, elk, and ostriches.

Goods and Services

A large portion of the workforce in Minnesota is employed in the manufacturing sector. Some of the state's most important manufactured goods include scientific instruments, computers, office equipment, medical devices, and electronic and electrical equipment. Minnesota factories also produce paper, transportation equipment, and food products.

The varied service sector of the economy employs the majority of all workers in the state. Many Minnesotans work in finance, insurance, trade, transportation, government, education, and health care. Minnesota's tourism industry also employs many workers in hotels and restaurants. Computer-related services and others involving high technology have become increasingly important to the state economy.

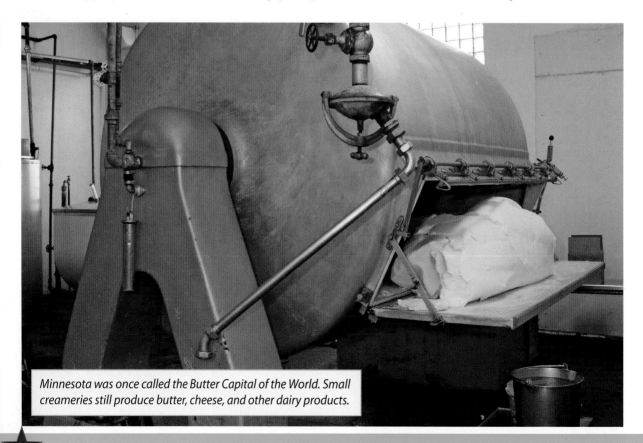

Minnesota was once called the Butter Capital of the World. Small creameries still produce butter, cheese, and other dairy products.

Minnesota's ports on Lake Superior handle millions of tons of freight every year.

With such a strong agricultural sector, Minnesota farmers have long formed **cooperatives** to help buy and sell their products. Today, the largest and most important consumer cooperatives in the state are the creameries. The creameries sell dairy products such as milk, butter, and cheese. Others cooperatives in Minnesota include worker cooperatives that provide resources to farmers.

Rivers were the first important mode for transporting people and goods in many parts of the state. **Barges** on the Mississippi River carry bulk products to and from the major inland ports at St. Paul and Minneapolis. The rail system of northeastern Minnesota brings iron ore and taconite products to the Lake Superior ports of Duluth and Superior, Wisconsin.

Years ago, Minnesota used waterpower to produce a great deal of its electricity. As industries grew, the need for power became too great for these plants. Today, most of Minnesota's electricity comes from plants that burn coal or natural gas, as well as from nuclear power plants.

American Indians

Evidence of humans living in the area that is now Minnesota dates back as much as 8,000 years. These earliest inhabitants were hunters who roamed from place to place. By about 1,000 years ago, woodland cultures were established in the region. The people from these cultures created permanent communities, farmed corn, beans, and squash, and built burial mounds of earth.

In the late 1600s, the Ojibwe, also called Chippewa, **migrated** into what is now Minnesota. The Dakota, also called Sioux, were already living around the Lake Superior region. After many wars, the Ojibwe drove the Dakota into the prairies of the southern and western parts of the Minnesota area. The Ojibwe then settled in the forest regions of northern and central Minnesota. They lived in permanent villages full of dome-shaped houses made from wood and birch bark. The women tended small gardens and gathered wild plants, while the men hunted and fished.

Dakota Chief Little Crow led his people in a rebellion against U.S. settlers in 1862.

Settlers began moving into the area in the mid-1800s, and they wanted the Indians' land. Both the Dakota and Ojibwe were forced to sign treaties that gave most of their land in Minnesota to the United States. The United States broke most of the promises it made to the Indians in these treaties. In 1862, the Dakota rose up against the settlers in the Minnesota River Valley. This uprising became one of the bloodiest wars between Indians and settlers in the country's history. The Dakota were defeated within a few weeks, and most of them were either captured or forced to flee the region. Today, most of the Ojibwe in Minnesota live in the Twin Cities area or in one of seven reservations in the north. The state's Dakota live mainly in four communities in the south.

Indians hunted and killed animals such as deer and bison. The hide was scraped clean and then stretched on wooden frames, before being used to make clothing, blankets, and tools.

I DIDN'T KNOW THAT!

Minnesota Indians constructed burial mounds that had a central chamber, containing the bodies of important people.

Many Ojibwe prefer to be called Anishinabe, which means "first people."

The name Chippewa most likely developed as a result of early settlers mispronouncing the name Ojibwe.

Indians painted images, called pictographs, on rocks. These images can still be seen today.

Indians from as far away as the Appalachians and the Rocky Mountains used to meet in a sacred place of peace in southwestern Minnesota. There, they dug up a hard red rock they used to make peace pipes.

Ojibwe used birch bark to make lightweight canoes and storage containers. They also covered their homes with birch bark or mats of woven reeds.

Explorers and Missionaries

In 1660, French fur traders Pierre Esprit Radisson and Médard Chouart, sieur des Groseilliers, were the first Europeans to visit what is now Minnesota. They explored the western portion of the Lake Superior area. In 1673, French explorers Father Jacques Marquette and Louis Joliet discovered the upper portion of the Mississippi River. Six years later, Daniel Greysolon, sieur du Lhut, entered the area by way of Lake Superior. He spent time with the Dakota near Mille Lacs and claimed much of what is now Minnesota for France. Later, the city of Duluth took its name from du Lhut.

Father Louis Hennepin was a French missionary sent to explore the upper Mississippi River. In 1680, he discovered and named St. Anthony Falls. Soon after Hennepin's discovery, the area became a favorite hunting ground for French fur traders. Hennepin, meanwhile, was captured by the Dakota and had to be rescued by Daniel Greysolon.

Fur trader René Boucher traveled to Minnesota in 1727 with a team of explorers. His expedition eventually arrived on the shore of Lake Pepin. A fort was built on the site and became known as Fort Beauharnois.

Pierre Esprit Radisson wrote about his travels in the region that became Minnesota. His description of the fur trade attracted others to the area.

Timeline of Settlement

Early Exploration

1660 French fur traders Pierre Esprit Radisson and Médard Chouart, sieur des Groseilliers, become the first Europeans to visit the area.

1673 Jacques Marquette and Louis Joliet discover the upper portion of the Mississippi River.

1679 Daniel Greysolon, sieur du Lhut, enters the area and spends time with the Dakota near Mille Lacs.

1680 Father Louis Hennepin explores the upper Mississippi River.

Settlements and U.S. Control

1727 Fort Beauharnois is built on the shore of Lake Pepin.

1783 After the American Revolution, the new United States gains what is now northeastern Minnesota from Great Britain.

1803 Most of what is now western and southern Minnesota becomes part of the United States as a result of President Thomas Jefferson's Louisiana Purchase of land from France.

1819 Fort St. Anthony is built, later renamed Fort Snelling.

1836 Minnesota is part of the Wisconsin Territory.

1837 Stillwater becomes one of the area's first cities, following the signing of treaties with the Indians.

1838 St. Paul is settled.

Territory and Statehood

1849 The Minnesota Territory is established.

1858 Minnesota becomes a state.

1862 Conflict breaks out between the Dakota Indians and the United States.

Early Settlers

The first permanent U.S. settlement in the region that became Minnesota was Fort St. Anthony, which was established in 1819. A few years later, it was renamed Fort Snelling in honor of Colonel Josiah Snelling, who built it. Settlement in the area grew in the following years.

Map of Settlements and Resources in Early Minnesota

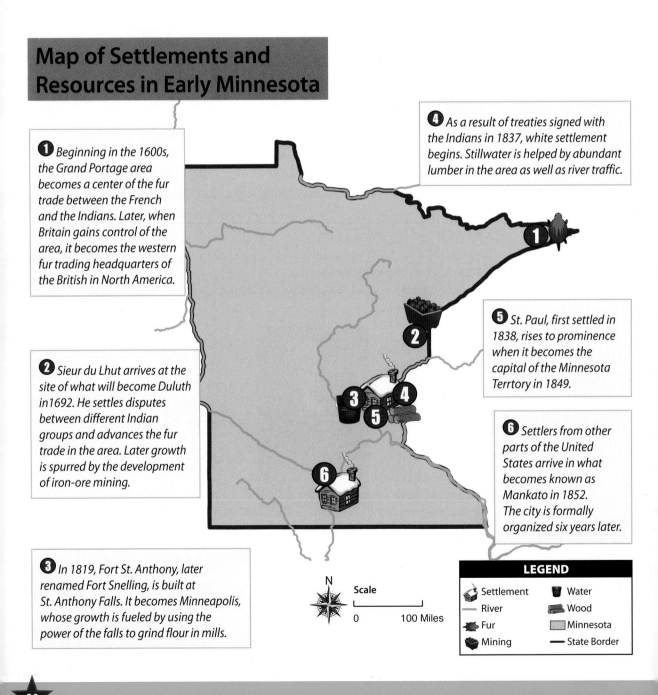

4 As a result of treaties signed with the Indians in 1837, white settlement begins. Stillwater is helped by abundant lumber in the area as well as river traffic.

1 Beginning in the 1600s, the Grand Portage area becomes a center of the fur trade between the French and the Indians. Later, when Britain gains control of the area, it becomes the western fur trading headquarters of the British in North America.

5 St. Paul, first settled in 1838, rises to prominence when it becomes the capital of the Minnesota Terrtory in 1849.

2 Sieur du Lhut arrives at the site of what will become Duluth in1692. He settles disputes between different Indian groups and advances the fur trade in the area. Later growth is spurred by the development of iron-ore mining.

6 Settlers from other parts of the United States arrive in what becomes known as Mankato in 1852. The city is formally organized six years later.

3 In 1819, Fort St. Anthony, later renamed Fort Snelling, is built at St. Anthony Falls. It becomes Minneapolis, whose growth is fueled by using the power of the falls to grind flour in mills.

N

Scale

0   100 Miles

LEGEND

🪙	Settlement	💧	Water
—	River	🪵	Wood
🐾	Fur	⬜	Minnesota
⛏	Mining	▬	State Border

During the middle of the 1800s, the U.S. government signed several treaties with American Indian groups, which turned over most of the Indians' land to the United States. Settlers then flocked to the Mississippi and Minnesota river valleys to farm the fertile soil. In 1858, Minnesota became a state.

Another rapid period of settlement in Minnesota occurred during the 1880s, when settlers rushed to claim land in the western and southwestern parts of the state. In the same period, lumbering was at its peak, and flour milling was becoming important. Both Minneapolis and the neighboring city of St. Paul tripled in population during the 1880s. Minneapolis was the state's lumber, milling, and retail center. St. Paul was the center of transportation, wholesaling, finance, and government. Railroads played a key role in the growth of these Twin Cities. In 1883, a great celebration marked the completion of the Northern Pacific Railway from St. Paul to the West Coast.

In 1880, the population of St. Paul was 41,473. It had more than tripled, to 133,156, by 1890.

Trading posts such as Grand Portage were important meeting places for early fur traders and travelers in the region.

Between 1853 and 1857, the number of people in Minnesota grew from 40,000 to 150,000.

Minnesota was the first state to send volunteers to fight for the Union in the Civil War. Some 24,000 people from Minnesota eventually fought in the Union Army.

In 1823, the first flour was milled at St. Anthony Falls.

Minnesota was part of the Wisconsin Territory, which was established in 1836. The Minnesota Territory was established in 1849.

Alexander Ramsey was the first territorial governor of Minnesota.

Notable People

Many notable Minnesotans contributed to the development of their state and country. While no U.S. presidents have come from the state, a number of vice presidents, Supreme Court justices, and other leaders have called Minnesota home.

WILLIAM O. DOUGLAS (1898–1980)

William O. Douglas was born in Maine Township. He practiced law and taught at different law schools. In the 1930s, he became one of President Franklin D. Roosevelt's advisers, and in 1939, he became a justice on the U.S. Supreme Court. During his time as a justice, Douglas was a strong defender of personal freedom and **First Amendment** rights. He retired from the Court in 1975. Douglas served on the Court for 36 years and 209 days, making him the longest serving justice in Supreme Court history. He also holds the records for the most opinions written and the most **dissents** written by any member of the Court.

WARREN BURGER (1907–1995)

Warren Burger was born in St. Paul and grew up on his family farm nearby. He worked his way through college at the University of Minnesota and later attended law school. Burger became a lawyer, got involved in politics, and became a judge. In 1969, he became chief justice of the U.S. Supreme Court, a position he filled until 1986. As chief justice, he preserved the power and authority of the Court. After his retirement from the Court, he led the campaign to mark the 1987 bicentennial of the U.S. Constitution.

HARRY BLACKMUN (1908–1999)

Harry Blackmun was born in Illinois and raised in St. Paul. Warren Burger was one of his childhood friends. Blackmun became a lawyer in Minnesota, then was named to the U.S. Supreme Court in 1970. He served on the Court until 1994, his opinions becoming increasingly liberal as the years went on.

HUBERT HUMPHREY (1911–1978)

Hubert Humphrey was born in South Dakota. He settled in Minnesota, where he was mayor of Minneapolis. As a liberal Democrat, he was elected to the U.S. Senate in 1948. He served in the Senate until January 1965, when he became U.S. vice president under Lyndon Johnson. Humphrey ran for the presidency himself in 1968 but lost. He was elected to the Senate again in 1970 and served there until his death.

WALTER MONDALE (1928–)

Walter Mondale was born in Ceylon. He graduated from the University of Minnesota Law School. In 1964, he became a U.S. senator from Minnesota. In January 1977, he became U.S. vice president under Jimmy Carter. Mondale ran for the presidency in 1984 but was defeated by Ronald Reagan.

William James Mayo (1861–1939) was born in Le Sueur and became a physician. He and his brother, Charles, founded a hospital in Rochester in 1889 that became the Mayo Clinic. Today, it is one of the world's leading health-care institutions.

Eugene McCarthy (1916–2005) was born in Watkins. He served in Congress, first in the House of Representatives and then in the Senate, from January 1949 to January 1971. He campaigned for the Democratic presidential nomination in 1968. Although he did not win the nomination, his campaign was widely considered to be a factor in President Lyndon Johnson's decision not to seek reelection.

Population

The total population of Minnesota was 5,303,925 at the time of the 2010 Census. More than 70 percent of Minnesotans live in towns or cities. The Twin Cities and their suburbs make up the major population center of the state, with about half of the state's residents living in the area. Duluth, Rochester, and St. Cloud are the main population centers outside the Twin Cities.

The vast majority of Minnesota's population is made up of people of European descent. About 4.7 percent of people in the state are African American, 4.3 percent are Hispanic, 3.8 percent are Asian, and 1.3 percent are American Indian. Most of the Indians in Minnesota are Ojibwe.

Minnesota Population 1950-2010

The population of Minnesota has grown in every decade since 1950 and is now more than 75 percent larger than in the mid-20th century. What kind of actions does a state need to take to deal with this type of population growth?

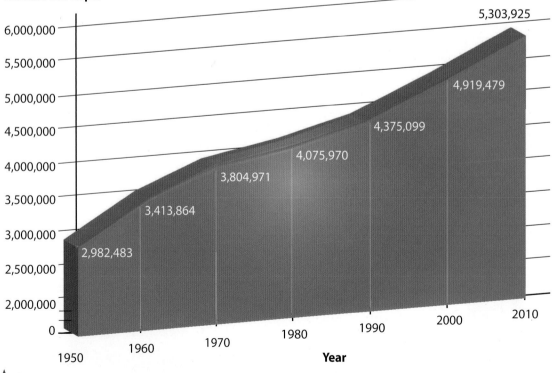

Number of People

- 6,000,000
- 5,500,000
- 5,000,000
- 4,500,000
- 4,000,000
- 3,500,000
- 3,000,000
- 2,500,000
- 2,000,000
- 0

5,303,925
4,919,479
4,375,099
4,075,970
3,804,971
3,413,864
2,982,483

1950 · 1960 · 1970 · 1980 · 1990 · 2000 · 2010

Year

There are approximately 1,990 public schools in Minnesota, with more than 52,000 full-time teachers. More than 820,000 students, in grades kindergarten through 12, attend these schools. Almost 88 percent of people in Minnesota, age 25 and over, graduated from high school. More than 28 percent of people in the state, age 25 and over, have a bachelor's degree or higher.

Minnesota's state college and university system is made up of 25 two-year colleges and seven state universities. The main University of Minnesota campus is in the Twin Cities. There are also private educational institutions in the state, such as Carlton College and St. Olaf College, both located in Northfield, and Macalester College, in St. Paul.

The city of Osseo hosts an annual marching band festival. Large crowds turn out to watch the competition between bands from high schools across the state and the Upper Midwest.

St. Cloud, located in the central part of the state, served as a refuge for fleeing settlers during the Dakota uprising of 1862.

Duluth, a port city on Lake Superior, occupies a narrow strip of land about 30 miles long that hugs the lake's shoreline.

Henry Wadsworth Longfellow's poem *The Song of Hiawatha* made Minnehaha Falls famous. The falls lie within the city limits of Minneapolis.

The University of Minnesota was founded in Minneapolis in 1851, seven years before Minnesota became a state.

The Minnesota State Capitol Building, where the state legislature meets, was opened in 1905. It took 12 years to plan and build.

Politics and Government

The Minnesota Territory was established in 1849, and Minnesota became the 32nd state in 1858. In 1857, a convention was held to draw up a constitution for the state. The Democratic and Republican parties were so divided that they drafted separate constitutions. After weeks of debate, they finally reached an agreement. Voters approved the new constitution that year.

The state government is divided into three branches. They are the executive, the legislative, and the judicial. The executive branch, led by the governor, is responsible for making sure the laws are carried out. The governor and lieutenant governor, along with other public servants such as the secretary of state and attorney general, serve four-year terms. The legislative branch is made up of two parts, the Senate and the House of Representatives. The state's 67 senators serve four-year terms, and its 134 representatives serve two-year terms. The legislative branch creates new laws and changes existing ones. The judicial branch consists of the state's courts. Minnesota's highest court is the seven-member Supreme Court. There are also lower-level courts, including courts in each of the state's 87 counties.

Comedian and author Al Franken, who was raised in Minnesota, was elected a U.S. senator from the state in a close election in 2008.

I DIDN'T KNOW THAT!

Minnesota's state song is called "Hail Minnesota."

Here are the words to the song:

Minnesota, hail to thee!
Hail to thee our state so dear!
Thy light shall ever be
A beacon bright and clear.
Thy sons and daughters true
Will proclaim thee near
* and far.*
They shall guard thy fame
And adore thy name;
Thou shalt be their
* Northern Star.*

Like the stream that bends
* to sea,*
Like the pine that seeks
* the blue,*
Minnesota, still for thee,
Thy sons are strong and true.
From thy woods and
* waters fair,*
From thy prairies waving far,
At thy call they throng,
With their shout and song,
Hailing thee their
* Northern Star.*

Cultural Groups

The rich farmlands and forests of Minnesota attracted settlers from all over the world. French Canadians and people from Sweden, Norway, Germany, and Ireland were some of Minnesota's first settlers of European heritage. They were soon joined by immigrants from Finland, Poland, and what are now the Czech Republic and Slovakia. A number of different ethnic festivals are held throughout the state each year. In April, St. Paul hosts a celebration of the state's ethnic diversity with the Festival of Nations. Each fall, New Prague holds a harvest festival called Dozinky, which celebrates the town's Czech heritage. The festival features Czech music, food, and arts and crafts, which are sold at an open-air market. Visitors to the annual Immigrant's Christmas, held in Annandale's Minnesota Pioneer Park, can learn about the holiday traditions of many of the state's ethnic groups.

The American Swedish Institute was founded in Minneapolis in 1929 by an immigrant named Swan Turnblad. He donated his mansion to serve as the institute's home.

Statues of the legendary logger Paul Bunyan and his pet blue ox, Babe, are a popular attraction in Bemidji.

BEMI
PAUL
BUNYAN
1937

The major areas of Swedish settlement in the state are immediately north of the Twin Cities and in scattered locations in west-central and northwestern Minnesota. The American Swedish Institute, in Minneapolis, runs a museum about the area's Swedish heritage. Traditional Swedish fiddling, dancing, folk costumes, crafts, games, and food are all part of the many festivals that the institute sponsors throughout the year.

Several American Indian groups in Minnesota hold annual powwows that feature drumming and different styles of Indian dancing. In September, a public powwow by the Dakota at Mankato celebrates their traditional ways. The annual powwow in Hinckley attracts Indians from all over the Midwest.

Arts and Entertainment

The Twin Cities area serves as the center of Minnesota's cultural institutions. The Minnesota Orchestra performs in Orchestra Hall in downtown Minneapolis. The hall is famous for the **acoustic** cubes on its ceiling and stage walls. These cubes deflect the sound throughout the hall so that the audience can hear the performance perfectly. Also located in Minneapolis is the Children's Theatre Company, which is nationally recognized as one of the finest of its kind. The Minnesota Dance Theatre is the most prominent resident dance company in the Twin Cities. The famous Guthrie Theater opened in Minneapolis in 1963. It is named after Sir Tyrone Guthrie, a British stage director and actor, who helped establish the theater company. There are several art galleries in Minnesota. Perhaps the best known is the Walker Art Center in Minneapolis, which opened in 1927 and since the 1940s has focused on modern art.

Actress and singer Judy Garland was born in Grand Rapids in 1922. She became a star when she appeared as Dorothy in the film The Wizard of Oz *in 1939.*

Many famous entertainers have come from Minnesota. They include James Arness, who starred in the TV show Gunsmoke for 20 years, Academy Award–winning actress Jessica Lange, who appeared in the movie *Tootsie*, is from Minnesota. So was Judy Garland, who starred in films such as *The Wizard of Oz*, *Meet Me in St. Louis*, and *A Star Is Born*. More recent stars from Minnesota include Josh Hartnett, T. R. Knight, and Jessica Biel. Ethan and Joel Coen, who together write, direct, and produce films, are from St. Louis Park. Singer and songwriter Bob Dylan was born in Duluth and raised in Hibbing.

Numerous writers can call Minnesota home. They include Sinclair Lewis, F. Scott Fitzgerald, Louis Erdrich, and children's author Maud Hart Lovelace, whose books were based on her own life growing up in Mankato. Garrison Keillor, who writes about life in the imaginary Lake Wobegon, hosts a popular radio program called *A Prairie Home Companion*.

I DIDN'T KNOW THAT!

Actress Winona Ryder, who was born in Olmsted County, was named after the nearby city of Winona.

The Minnesota Opera, founded in 1963, is part of the Walker Art Center.

The Minneapolis Symphony Orchestra was founded in 1903.

Pop-star Prince was born in Minneapolis, where he still lives.

Minneapolis-born cartoonist Charles M. Schulz created the "Charlie Brown" comic strip. He grew up in St. Paul and began his career there.

The Coen brothers, Ethan and Joel, grew up in a Minneapolis suburb. They have written, directed, and produced numerous movies together, including True Grit in 2010.

Sports

Minnesota is the place to be for professional sports. The Twin Cities boast five major professional sports teams in four different sports. The Minnesota Vikings play in the National Football League. The Minnesota Twins, who play in baseball's American League, have twice won the World Series, in 1987 and 1991. There are currently two professional basketball teams, the Timberwolves in the National Basketball Association and the Lynx in the Women's National Basketball Association. The Minnesota Wild have competed in the National Hockey League since 2000.

High schools, colleges, and universities throughout the state have very active sports programs. Students in these programs compete in all kinds of events throughout the year. The Golden Gophers sports teams of the University of Minnesota have won national championships over the years in various sports, including football, baseball, wrestling, and both men's and women's ice hockey.

Minnesota Twins catcher Joe Mauer was born in St. Paul. He has played his entire professional career with the Twins and has a lifetime batting average, through the 2010 season, of .327.

Snowboarding is just one of the many winter sports that are popular in Minnesota. The state's many hills and cold, snowy weather also lead many to hit the slopes and trails on skis, snowshoes, and snowmobiles.

With so many well-stocked lakes and streams in the state, Minnesotans never run out of places to fish. The many bodies of water offer other activities as well, such as waterskiing, kayaking, canoeing, motorboating, and inner-tubing. Outdoor sports are not limited to the summer. Popular winter sports in Minnesota include skiing, snowboarding, snowmobiling, snowshoeing, and dog sledding. Minnesota is the envy of the nation when it comes to cross-country ski and snowmobile trails. The largest and highest downhill ski area in the Midwest is found at Spirit Mountain, near Duluth.

I DIDN'T KNOW THAT!

Baseball great Roger Maris held the single-season home-run title for nearly 37 years, after hitting 61 homers in 1961. He was born in Hibbing.

Many members of the U.S. men's ice-hockey team that won the 1980 Olympic gold medal were from the University of Minnesota, as was the team's coach, Herb Brooks.

Minnesota has hundreds of miles of hiking trails, many of which wind along the lakes and rivers.

Cyclists enjoy 56 paved bike trails totaling some 1,288 miles along old railroad beds. Minnesota has more paved rail-to-trail bikeways than any other state in the country.

Golf is a popular pastime in Minnesota, with 575 golf courses in the state.

Rushing Rapids Parkway is where the St. Louis River thunders through a rocky gorge and over slabs of ancient rock. Whitewater rafting is the only way one can get through these rapids.

Waterskiing was invented in 1922 on Lake Pepin, along the Mississippi River.

National Averages Comparison

The United States is a federal republic, consisting of fifty states and the District of Columbia. Alaska and Hawai'i are the only non-contiguous, or non-touching, states in the nation. Today, the United States of America is the third-largest country in the world in population. The United States Census Bureau takes a census, or count of all the people, every ten years. It also regularly collects other kinds of data about the population and the economy. How does Minnesota compare to the national average?

Comparison Chart

United States 2010 Census Data *	USA	Minnesota
Admission to Union	NA	May 11, 1858
Land Area (in square miles)	3,537,438.44	79,610.08
Population Total	308,745,538	5,303,925
Population Density (people per square mile)	87.28	66.62
Population Percentage Change (April 1, 2000, to April 1, 2010)	9.7%	7.8%
White Persons (percent)	72.4%	85.3%
Black Persons (percent)	12.6%	5.2%
American Indian and Alaska Native Persons (percent)	0.9%	1.1%
Asian Persons (percent)	4.8%	4.0%
Native Hawaiian and Other Pacific Islander Persons (percent)	0.2%	—
Some Other Race (percent)	6.2%	1.9%
Persons Reporting Two or More Races (percent)	2.9%	2.4%
Persons of Hispanic or Latino Origin (percent)	16.3%	4.7%
Not of Hispanic or Latino Origin (percent)	83.7%	95.3%
Median Household Income	$52,029	$57,318
Percentage of People Age 25 or Over Who Have Graduated from High School	80.4%	87.9%

*All figures are based on the 2010 United States Census, with the exception of the last two items. Percentages may not add to 100 because of rounding.

How to Improve My Community

S trong communities make strong states. Think about what features are important in your community. What do you value? Education? Health? Forests? Safety? Beautiful spaces? Government works to help citizens create ideal living conditions that are fair to all by providing services in communities. Consider what changes you could make in your community. How would they improve your state as a whole? Using this concept web as a guide, write a report that outlines the features you think are most important in your community and what improvements could be made. A strong state needs strong communities.

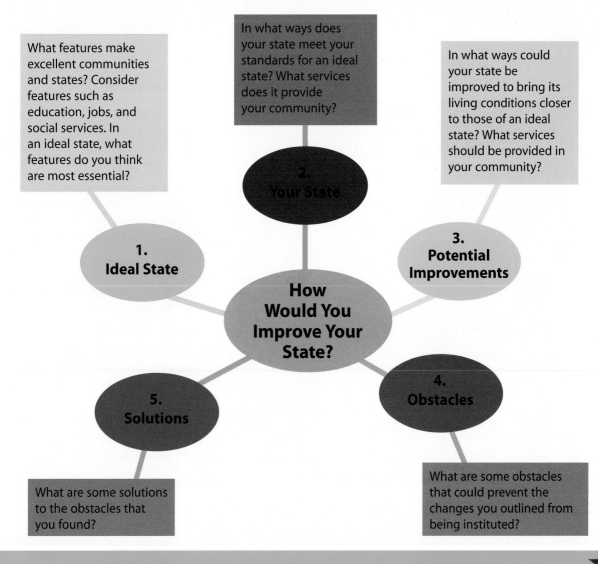

What features make excellent communities and states? Consider features such as education, jobs, and social services. In an ideal state, what features do you think are most essential?

In what ways does your state meet your standards for an ideal state? What services does it provide your community?

In what ways could your state be improved to bring its living conditions closer to those of an ideal state? What services should be provided in your community?

2.
Your State

1.
Ideal State

3.
Potential Improvements

How Would You Improve Your State?

4.
Obstacles

5.
Solutions

What are some solutions to the obstacles that you found?

What are some obstacles that could prevent the changes you outlined from being instituted?

Exercise Your Mind!

Think about these questions and then use your research skills to find the answers and learn more fascinating facts about Minnesota. A teacher, librarian, or parent may be able to help you locate the best sources to use in your research.

1 Does wild rice grow naturally in Minnesota?

2 The state bird is the common loon. How many loons make their home in Minnesota each year?

3 What is the elevation of the lowest point in Minnesota, on the shore of Lake Superior?

a. 0 feet (sea level)
b. 327 feet
c. 602 feet
d. 1,028 feet

4 True or False? The Metrodome is the only arena to have hosted the World Series, the Super Bowl, and the college basketball Final Four.

5 Roger Maris was born in Minnesota and held the major league baseball home-run crown from 1961 until 1998. How many home runs did he hit?

6 At one time Minnesota was completely covered by a single lake. What was the lake's name?

a. Lake Superior
b. Lake Agassiz
c. Lake of the Woods
d. Leech Lake

7 The author of the famous novel *The Great Gatsby* was born in St. Paul. Can you name the writer?

8 Minnesota hockey player Scott Olson, wanting to train during the summer months, invented what popular recreation in 1980?

Words to Know

acoustic: of or relating to sound or hearing

barges: flat-bottomed boats used on canals and rivers to carry goods

bogs: areas of wet, spongy ground

coniferous forests: forests with primarily cone-bearing and needle-leaved trees

cooperatives: businesses owned by their members with profits shared between them

deciduous forests: forests with primarily broad-leaved trees that lose their leaves every year

dissents: opinions issued by a judge that do not agree with the opinion of the majority of judges

endangered: in danger of dying out

First Amendment: an amendment to the U.S. Constitution that protects freedom of religion, speech, assembly, or petition

flour milling: grinding and sifting wheat, rye, and other grains into flour for making bread and cakes

glaciers: large masses of slow-moving ice

metropolitan areas: a city and its surrounding suburbs and towns

migrated: moved from one place to another

open-pit mines: huge holes in the ground where minerals are mined, loaded into trucks, and hauled away for processing

species: a group of animals or plants that share the same characteristics and can mate

Index

Log on to www.av2books.com

AV² by Weigl brings you media enhanced books that support active learning. Go to www.av2books.com, and enter the special code found on page 2 of this book. You will gain access to enriched and enhanced content that supplements and complements this book. Content includes video, audio, web links, quizzes, a slide show, and activities.

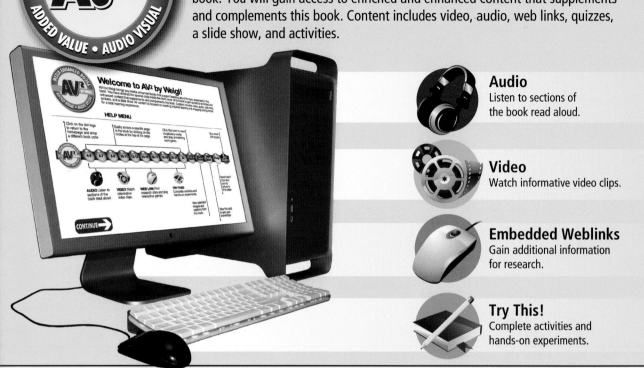

Audio
Listen to sections of the book read aloud.

Video
Watch informative video clips.

Embedded Weblinks
Gain additional information for research.

Try This!
Complete activities and hands-on experiments.

WHAT'S ONLINE?

Try This!	Embedded Weblinks	Video	EXTRA FEATURES
Test your knowledge of the state in a mapping activity.	Discover more attractions in Minnesota.	Watch a video introduction to Minnesota.	**Audio** Listen to sections of the book read aloud.
Find out more about precipitation in your city.	Learn more about the history of the state.	Watch a video about the features of the state.	**Key Words** Study vocabulary, and complete a matching word activity.
Plan what attractions you would like to visit in the state.	Learn the full lyrics of the state song.		**Slide Show** View images and captions, and prepare a presentation.
Learn more about the early natural resources of the state.			**Quizzes** Test your knowledge.
Write a biography about a notable resident of Minnesota.			
Complete an educational census activity.			

AV² was built to bridge the gap between print and digital. We encourage you to tell us what you like and what you want to see in the future.

Sign up to be an AV² Ambassador at www.av2books.com/ambassador.

Due to the dynamic nature of the Internet, some of the URLs and activities provided as part of AV² by Weigl may have changed or ceased to exist. AV² by Weigl accepts no responsibility for any such changes. All media enhanced books are regularly monitored to update addresses and sites in a timely manner. Contact AV² by Weigl at 1-866-649-3445 or av2books@weigl.com with any questions, comments, or feedback.